D0836906

what the Bible
has to say about:

love

ISBN 0-687-07542-4

Scripture quotations are taken from the HOLY BIBLE, NEW
INTERNATIONAL VERSION ®. Copyright © 1973, 1978, 1984
International Bible Society.

Original edition published in English under the title
What God Has to Say About: Love by John Hunt Publishing Ltd,
New Alresford, Hants, UK.

This book was conceived, designed, and produced by

THE PALM PRESS

The Old Candlemakers, West Street
Lewes, East Sussex BN7 2NZ, UK

Creative Director: PETER BRIDGEWATER

Publisher: SOPHIE COLLINS

Editorial Director: STEVE LUCK

Designer: ANDREW MILNE

Project Editor: MANDY GREENFIELD

03 04 05 06 07 08 09 10 11 12 — 10 9 8 7 6 5 4 3 2 1

Manufactured in China

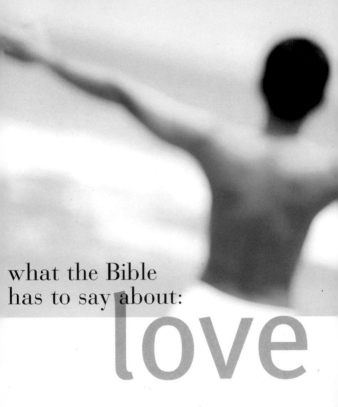

what the Bible has to say about:
love

Mark Water

DIMENSIONS
FOR LIVING
NASHVILLE

God is love.

Whoever

lives in

love lives

in God, and

God in him.

1 John 4: 16

Introduction We all know the saying that it is love that makes the world go round. Love is at the heart of everything good in life. But it can be hard to find. And it can come and go.

There are a couple of seemingly insurmountable problems that face us as we think about how loving or unloving we are.

Problem number one is trying to define the word. There are numerous different meanings of the single English word "love." Part 3 of this book, "The Four Loves," explores four of the common meanings we give to the word.

Problem number two is much tougher. The biggest problem about love is our inability to be loving. We feel that we just never show the kind of love we want to, or that God wants of us.

So what are we to do? The answer the Bible supplies is simple, yet profound. It is, however, one that takes effort and humility to put into practice. We are to recall that we are loved by God. The more we meditate on this, the more we will know our loving heavenly Father. And when we begin to grasp a little of the immense love of God the Father, we will then begin to behave like his children. The roots of love are found in God and not in ourselves.

For God so loved the world that he gave his one and only Son, that whoever believes in him shall not perish but have eternal life.

John 3: 16

contents

Part 1
Loving
Ourselves

8

Introduction "Love your neighbor as yourself," said Jesus. But suppose we don't love ourselves? And what does Jesus mean by "love"? Maybe my idea of "love" is so mistaken that I've no hope of loving my neighbor.

Psychologists tell us that we can't love others without loving ourselves. If we don't like ourselves, we have nothing to give. Jesus said, "'Love the Lord your God with all your heart and with all your soul and with all your mind.' This is the first and greatest commandment. And the second is like it: 'Love your neighbor as yourself.'" Matthew 22: 37–39.

When we have tackled the first command, to love God with our whole being, we find we are released from our self-centeredness and are enabled to love ourselves from a God-centered perspective. This new self, rooted in the love of God, enables us to "love our neighbor as ourselves." We love God in the love of God. We long for God in others as we long for him in ourselves.

Then God said, "Let us make man in our

image, in our likeness." Genesis 1: 26

In God's

Love has something to do with respect. But why should I respect myself? Genesis 1 gives the reason: God has made me in his image and likeness. God made human beings to be like him in a way that nothing else in creation is like him. To use computer terminology, Homo sapiens *is compatible with God.*

image

A fractured image

12

Genesis 1: 31 says: "God saw all that he had made, and it was very good." And that includes human beings. What went wrong? The first human beings rebelled against God. They introduced the virus of original sin into Homo sapiens. God's image in us is tarnished. But original sin is washed away by baptism.

The evil I do not want to do—

this I keep on doing. Romans 7: 19

Some years ago in the correspondence columns of The Times *different views were expressed on the question of what's wrong with the world. Then there came a letter that said:*

>*"Dear Sir,*
>
>*What's wrong with the world?*
>
>*I am.*
>
>*Yours faithfully,*
>
>*G. K. Chesterton"*

But it's God who has the last word on this subject. He says, "I know all about you, and I still love you."

The
last
word

This is love: not that we loved God, but that he loved us and sent his Son as an atoning sacrifice for our sins.

1 John 4: 10

God's love

The surprising truth is that we are the object of God's love. The God whose power made the universe loves us and his love will never change, no matter what we do. Not that this means that we can do what we please! But we know that because of the life and death on the Cross of Jesus Christ, sinners are redeeemed and we are always loved by God.

17

for us

18

Jesus said, "Greater love has no one than this, that he lay down his life for his friends." John 15: 13

True love is not sloppy, or sentimental, or indulgent, or well-intentioned but weak, or kindly but distant. It's powerful and active, intelligent and present. True love means wanting—and acting to bring about—God's best for someone, including God's best for me. That's the kind of love we see in Jesus Christ, and it means giving myself up to God.

19

Transforming love

*Jesus said to him,
"Today salvation has
come to this house,
because this man, too,
is a son of Abraham.
For the Son of Man
came to seek and to
save what was lost."*

Luke 19: 9, 10

Zacchaeus was a tax collector who used extortion to fill his coffers. One day Jesus invited himself to a meal at Zacchaeus' house. Afterwards Zacchaeus declared to the astonished citizens of Jericho, "I'll give away half my riches, and if I've defrauded anyone, I'll pay back four times what I took." When we, like Zacchaeus, know that God loves us, we are empowered to love others.

Part 2
God Loving Us

22

Introduction For Christians it's receiving the love of God that enables us to love. The more we can receive, the more we can give.

This idea of God loving us may be fairly new to us, or it may be one that we have grown up with since childhood. Either way, it's possible that we have become so familiar with it that we almost ignore it. We must freshen up!

First, we remember who spoke about God's love for us. Second, we recall just how much God loves us in Jesus. Jesus taught about God's love. We look to the Son of God himself, not some mere human guru, to reassure ourselves about God's love for us.

Then, we wonder at the extent of God's love for us. God loves us as much as he loved Jesus. "As the Father has loved me," Jesus explained to his first disciples, "so have I loved you." John 15: 9

Thank God for his love.

How Go

When they came to the place called the Skull, there they crucified him, along with the criminals—one on his right, the other on his left. Luke 23: 33

The best way to view God's love for us is to look at the Cross. Jesus' crucifixion is a picture of the length and height and depth of God's love. There we view no mere stoical martyr, but God himself dying for the sins of the world. In his prayer in Ephesians 3, Paul describes the vastness of God's love.

John, one of Jesus' apostles, known as the "apostle of love," wrote his Gospel to help his readers come to believe in Jesus and Jesus' great love. In his first letter, 1 John, he writes to assure his readers about God's love. He wants them to know for certain that God loves them.

I write these things to you who believe in the name of the Son of God so that you may know that you have eternal life.   1 John 5: 13

Assurance
of love

Patient love

But for that very reason I was shown mercy so that in me, the worst of sinners, Christ Jesus might display his unlimited patience as an example for those who would believe on him and receive eternal life.

1 Timothy 1: 16

Paul knew about God's love and God's patience at first hand. He started off as the first and worst persecutor of the early Christians, searching them out and having them dumped in prison. But after his heart and mind were bowled over by God's love he wrote to Timothy about God's "unlimited patience." God patiently seeks each person's salvation.

God's amazing love

But God demonstrates his own love for us in this: While we were still sinners, Christ died for us. Romans 5: 8

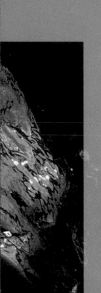

God's love for us is not dependent on our love for him. During Jesus' life on earth he was let down by Peter many times. Three times Peter denied ever even knowing Jesus. But did Jesus stop loving Peter? Of course not. We may often let Jesus down, but this does not mean that God has ceased to love us.

Forgiving

Have mercy on me, O God,

according to your unfailing love;

according to your great compassion

blot out my transgressions. Psalm 51: 1

David was Israel's greatest king. But he was by no means perfect. But when he did wrong, he confessed his sin to God and then experienced God's forgiveness. After he had committed adultery with Bathsheba and had her husband, Uriah, killed in battle, David cried out to God in Psalm 51. In repentance, we find healing and restoration in the love of God.

love

Part 3
The Four Loves

Introduction There are so many types of love. In his book, *The Four Loves*, C. S. Lewis summarized the four kinds of love that are seen in the Bible. Explaining the New Testament word for love, he wrote, "It is called *agape* in the New Testament to distinguish it from *eros* (sexual love), *storge* (family affection), and *philia* (friendship). So there are four kinds of love, all good in their proper place, but *agape* is the best because it is the kind God has for us and is good in all circumstances."

The writers of the New Testament wanted to write about God's love. But they did not want to use a word for love that could be confused with the pagan ideas of love, which were self-centered and based on self-gratification. So they turned to the little-used classical Greek word for love, *agape*, as their word for God-like love.

Eros, *storge*, and *philia* are all natural, even to people who know little about the love of God. But *agape*-love is not. All four are given by God, but are often misused or not used at all. But *agape* may be almost absent in our lives until God's grace renews us.

How beautiful you are and

how pleasing,

O love, with your delights!

Song of Songs 7: 6

The New Testament does not use the Greek word eros. *In the Greek and Roman world* eros *had become so badly debased into lust that the writers of the New Testament avoided using the word altogether. However, sexual love, beautifully depicted in the Old Testament's Song of Songs, is a gift of God and is to be respected and used selflessly.*

As a mother comforts her child,

so will I comfort you.

Isaiah 66: 13

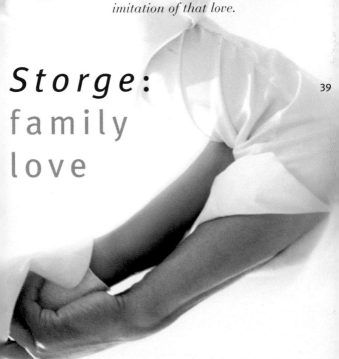

Storge was used of the natural affection between a parent and a child. This is frequently portrayed in the Bible as God's gift, and even as a characteristic of God himself. Children often first learn of love through the parent and we teach children of God's love by our own imitation of that love.

Storge:
family
love

"*I grieve for you, Jonathan my brother;*

you were very dear to me.

Your love for me was wonderful,

more wonderful than that of women."

2 Samuel 1: 26

The affection between friends like Jonathan and David is called philia. This kind of love can be between people of the same sex, as it was also in the case of Paul and Timothy. In times of war, people give up their lives for others. In everyday life we can give up our own lives in favor of a friend.

Philia:
love between friends

Agape: God's love

And now these three remain: faith, hope, and love. But the greatest of these is love.

1 Corinthians 13: 13

Agape *is God-like love, and is like no other love.* Agape *flows from a heart of love. The source of* agape *is God. Jesus is the pattern and inspiration of* agape. *It is pure, full of grace, mercy, and truth. Our love for God and for other people is meant to be* agape-love. *This abiding love never dies. It goes on past death into eternal life. This love is God.*

43

Part 4
Love and Sex

Introduction Sadly, Christians are often justly attacked for their attitude toward sex. The puritanical, prudish, and old-fashioned attitude toward sex that Christians are supposed to have is often lampooned by the press.

But the basic teaching of the Bible on this subject is positive: sexual love in marriage is one of God's greatest gifts. We should be thanking God for the gift of sex rather than entertaining any selfish thoughts about it. Part of the problem is solved as we remedy our ignorance about the Bible's teaching on this subject. Francis A. Schaeffer once wrote, "How often do Christians think of sexual matters as something second-rate. Never, never, never should we do so, according to the word of God."

Sex that is not rooted in the love of God can lead to harmful acts. Love that is self-righteous can lead to unkindness. Christians thank God for the gift of sex and ensure that it is never isolated from the whole teaching of the Bible on love.

"For some are eunuchs because they were born that way; others were made that way by men; and others have renounced marriage because of the kingdom of heaven."

Matthew 19: 12

Should

The Bible teaches that most people marry. Jesus taught that some people should forgo marriage. Marriage is not superior, nor the ultimate status for life, wonderful as it is. Paul writes that single people are able to devote themselves to God's work in a way that married people cannot.

everyone **marry?**

The arrows of Eros

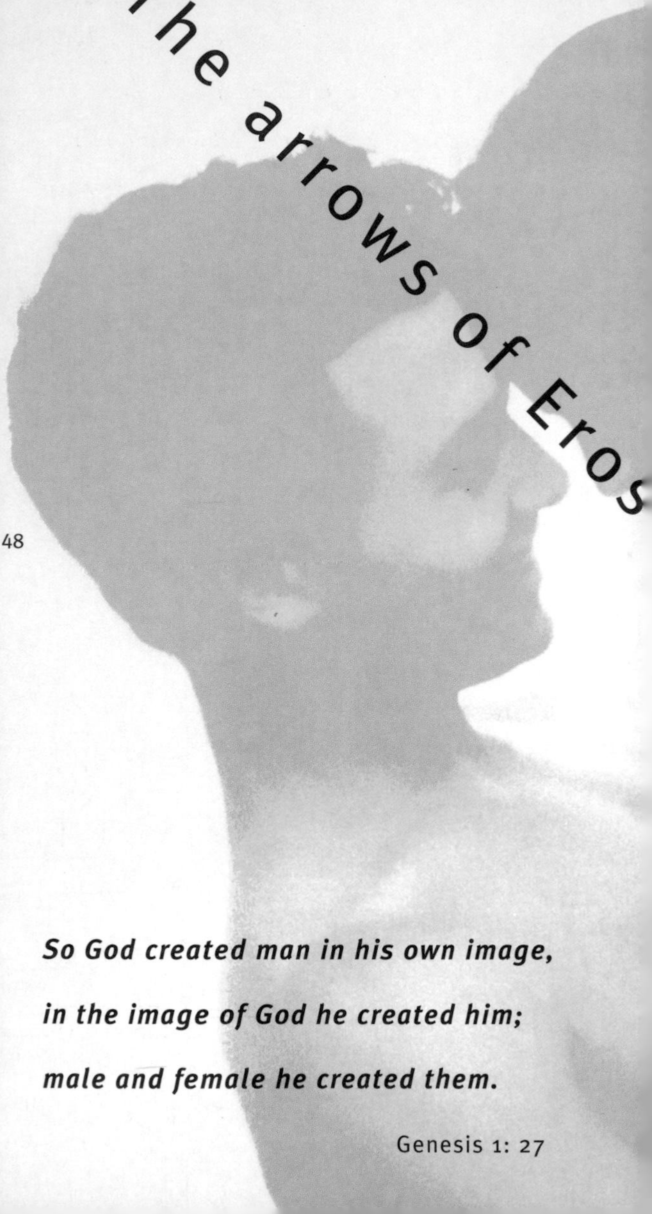

48

So God created man in his own image,

in the image of God he created him;

male and female he created them.

Genesis 1: 27

When Eros shoots his arrows, two people fall madly in love. Christians affirm that this is how our kind and loving Creator made us: that our capacity to have a fulfilling and sexual relationship comes from God himself. This sexual relationship is one part of that open and clear commitment to a lifelong partnership that is the basis of marriage.

Sex was never meant to end in the heartache of unwanted teenage pregnancies, in the trauma of abortion, or in the spread of sexually transmitted diseases, including AIDS. Humans bear the stamp of God. We transcend our base instincts to create a peaceful and stable world where the characteristics of peace and the divine life can flourish.

Sex

God blessed them and said to them,

"Be fruitful and increase in number."

Genesis 1: 28

vithout love

Is casual sex okay?

The body is not meant for sexual immorality, but for the Lord, and the Lord for the body.

1 Corinthians 6: 13

God's guidelines about sexual behavior are for our own good. Marital sex is the framework for responsible parenthood. Engaging in sexual activity is to be seen in the light of Christian responsibility. Casual sex is not okay with God, because it denies the selfless love that the permanent commitment of marriage brings.

You shall not commit adultery.

Exodus 20: 14

Sex with anyone other than a married partner is out for a Christian. What is now called an "affair" the Bible calls adultery. Adultery is a synonym for waywardness from God: God's people, Israel, are repeatedly accused of adultery. Faithfulness, loyalty, and commitment are the hallmarks of a godly life.

Loving more than one

Sex and children

For this reason a man will leave his father and mother and be united to his wife, and they will become one flesh.

Genesis 2: 24

The book of Genesis states that the propagation of the human race comes through the sexual relationship between male and female. Children are a blessing given by God. Marriage provides the stable home environment in which children can flourish.

May your fountain be blessed,

and may you rejoice in the wife of your youth.

A loving doe, a graceful deer—

may her breasts satisfy you always,

may you ever be captivated by her love.

Proverbs 5: 18, 19

Is sex for

These verses in Proverbs give a clear answer to the question "Is sex for our enjoyment?" Then there are eight erotic love poems in the Song of Songs!

enjoyment?

Don't refuse each other

Do not deprive each other except by mutual consent and for a time, so that you may devote yourselves to prayer.

1 Corinthians 7: 5

Paul tells the married Christians who live in the sex-mad city of Corinth: husbands, fulfill your marital duty to your wives; wives, you do the same. Sex in marriage is to be enjoyed. Couples should not deprive one another of sexual fulfillment, except by mutual consent, for a limited time, and for a good reason, such as prayer. Paul ranked prayer above sex!

> *I have been reminded of your sincere faith, which first lived in your grandmother Lois and in your mother Eunice and, I am persuaded, now lives in you also.*

2 Timothy 1: 5

Happy families

Families are environments where all members enjoy being loved. Paul mentions how blessed Timothy should count himself. For he had both a godly mother and grandmother. The ideal for any Christian family is parents who love God and live in love for others, for whom these two commandments of Jesus are the twin towers of their world.

Should children come first?

"Can a mother forget the baby at her breast and have no compassion on the child she has borne? Though she may forget, I will not forget you!"

Isaiah 49: 15

The short answer is "Yes!" Unconditional love is the key to bringing up children. Marriage is not about self-indulgence, but about Christ-like love. Christ loved the church and gave himself up for it. In our society, in which so many children are abused and neglected, marginalized even by their own families, the importance of sacrificial love for one's own children cannot be overemphasized.

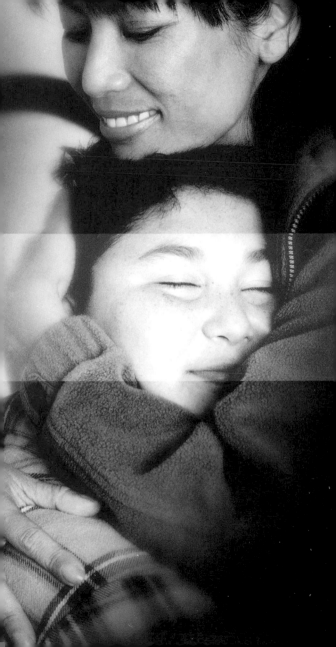

"I tell you that anyone who divorces his wife, except for marital unfaithfulness, causes her to become an adulteress, and anyone who marries the divorced woman commits adultery." Matthew 5: 32

So what happens when love grows cold? A failed marriage is just as tragic for Christians as it is for anyone else. Divorce is not a blanket solution to be applied to every situation. It is falling below God's standard. Nobody relishes a divorce. But no divorce need be the end of a fulfilling life.

Falling out
of love

Part 5
Love for
the World

Introduction Christians have sometimes been accused of cutting themselves off from the problems of the world, of focusing on the glory to come, and of being so heavenly minded that they are no earthly use. But that is a parody of the teaching of the Bible, and is an insult to most Christians.

Hospitals, schools for the poor, and relief agencies were first set up by Christians who knew that it was their Christian duty and calling to look after the whole person.

Preaching the gospel includes fighting the injustices in this world, as we see from the Old Testament prophets, and from Jesus himself.

It was Jesus' disciple, James, who wrote, "What good is it, my brothers, if a man claims to have faith but has no deeds? Can such faith save him? Suppose a brother or sister is without clothes and daily food. If one of you says to him, 'Go, I wish you well; keep warm and well fed,' but does nothing about his physical needs, what good is it? In the same way, faith by itself, if it is not accompanied by action, is dead." James 2: 14–17

"*Do not seek revenge or bear a grudge against one of your people, but love your neighbor as yourself. I am the Lord.*"

Leviticus 19: 18

Loving one's neighbor does not mean that we have to be inside each other's homes every day. Rather, loving our neighbors stems from having the right attitude toward them. It means not engaging in anything that may harm others, and this includes gossip. Christians should be concerned about another's well-being, not his or her downfall.

"Do not mistreat an alien or oppress him, for you were aliens in Egypt. Do not take advantage of a widow or an orphan." Exodus 22: 21, 22

Loving the

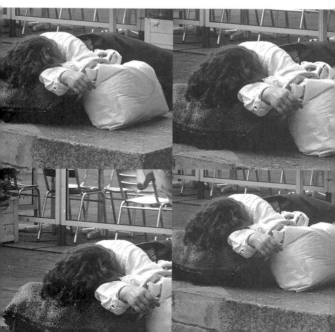

The Bible is on the side of the poor and the disadvantaged. So Christians should be in the fore-front of showing extra-special care for the disabled and the marginalized. Christians are expected to be compassionate, kind, and caring for all people, irrespective of race, color, or creed.

disadvantaged

If I give all I possess to the poor and surrender my body to the flames, but have not love, I gain nothing.

1 Corinthians 13: 3

Loving people

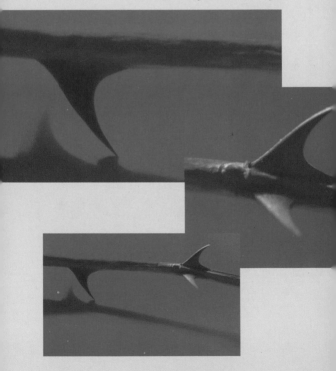

we don't like

Love is about wanting the best for somebody else. It's possible to go through life gritting one's teeth, as it were, doing the right thing, and smiling at everyone in sight, and yet have a bitter and twisted heart. A forgiving heart is one that is healed by the Lord. Only a heart full of divine love will succeed here.

But how is it to your credit

if you receive a beating for

doing wrong and endure it?

But if you suffer for doing

good and you endure it, this

is commendable before God.

1 Peter 2: 20

Loving people who may harm us

Unjust suffering can bear fruit for God. This is impossible without God's grace. A life in God is hard. We are expected to pick up our cross daily and follow Jesus. The joy is that God promises to daily bear our burdens.

Loving enemies

"You have heard that it was said, 'Love your neighbor and hate your enemy.' But I tell you: Love your enemies and pray for those who persecute you." Matthew 5: 43, 44

To the Jews of Jesus' day, "loving your neighbor" meant "love your fellow Jew." They even had a favorite saying, "Love your neighbor and hate your enemy." But this teaching is not found in the Old Testament. And Jesus taught his followers, not to seek revenge, but to love everyone, even hated enemies. Only God in us can do this.

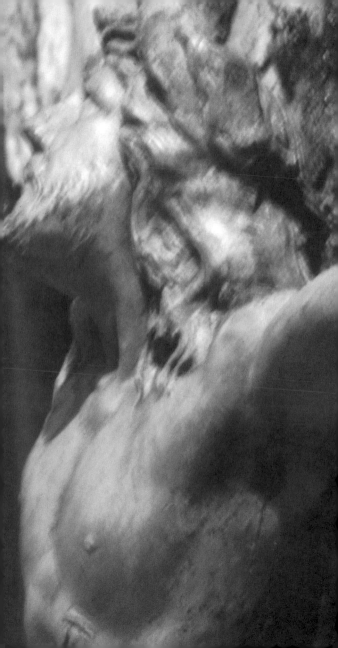

Hospitality

Do not forget to entertain strangers, for by so doing some people have entertained angels without knowing it. Hebrews 13: 2

One of the most practical ways of showing love is by sharing. One of the greatest things strangers appreciate is being warmly welcomed into a home. We should include people who may never return such an invitation to us. Modern-day wining and dining are not the yardsticks by which to measure Christian hospitality!

This is how we know what love is: Jesus Christ laid down his life for us. And we ought to lay down our lives for our brothers.

1 John 3: 16

When it comes to loving other people, Christians know that Jesus has set us an incredibly high standard. We should live with total self-sacrifice. But how can we ever achieve such a high ideal? Every selfless act is an example of "being perfect as our Father in heaven is perfect." We must persevere, since this is our goal.

Loving sacrificially

Our worldview needs to be broader than the following prayer: "Dear God, bless mommy and daddy, my sister and me, us four and not more." But it's a good start! Our own small world is a microcosm of the world at large. Charity begins at home. And we can practice these Christian acts of love anywhere.

Loving the

world

"'I needed clothes and you clothed me, I was sick and you looked after me, I was in prison and you came to visit me.'" Matthew 25: 36

Loving God's creatures

What about animal welfare? Should we care about how chickens are raised? Is it right for Christians to criticize some of the farming practices that involve animals being kept in harsh or cruel conditions? The principle here is that just as God shows his loving care to his creatures, so should we.

Every animal of the forest is mine,

and the cattle on a thousand hills.

I know every bird in the mountains,

and the creatures of the field are mine.

Psalm 50: 10, 11

Loving God's creation

The highest heavens belong to the Lord,

but the earth he has given to man.

Psalm 115: 16

Should Christians be green? If there had been no demand for hardwood, the rainforests would never have been decimated. Illegal logging would never have started. Psalm 115 states that not only is the Lord the Creator, but he has passed on to us the responsibility for caring for his creation. But we are only tenants, the Lord remains landlord.

Love in the church

"By this all men will know that you are my disciples, if you love one another."

John 13: 35

How do outsiders view Christians? How do non-churchgoers view us? Disunity and rows have divided Christians for far too long. Working positively together for unity among Christians honors God. There is one characteristic that Jesus kept on saying should be the hallmark of all his followers: we are to show love to each other.

> *"'For I was hungry and you gave me something to eat, I was thirsty and you gave me something to drink.'"*
>
> Matthew 25: 35

Loving future

Why not just quietly live for number one? Because Jesus came to put an end to sorrow and suffering, to death itself. Our actions demonstrate our solidarity with Jesus when we act like him. Selfless love given today can influence countless people, even those who are as yet unborn.

generations

A universe of love

How great is the love the Father has lavished on us, that we should be called children of God!
And that is what we are!

1 John 3: 1

Writers in every century have struggled to express the extent and power of God's unimaginable love. The love that "stands the test," as the hymn goes, is stronger than death, for it redeems and transforms us into the likeness of God himself—as his beloved children.

Mini Bible study The Bible verses that are quoted throughout this book are listed below. A straightforward way of having a Bible study is to look up each verse and note its significance in relation to the context in which it was originally set.

Genesis 1: 26
Genesis 1: 27
Genesis 1: 28
Genesis 1: 31
Genesis 2: 24
Exodus 20: 14
Exodus 22: 21, 22
Leviticus 19: 18
2 Samuel 1: 26
Psalm 50: 10, 11
Psalm 51: 1
Psalm 115: 16
Proverbs 5: 18, 19
Song of Songs 7: 6
Isaiah 49: 15
Isaiah 66: 13
Matthew 5: 32
Matthew 5: 43, 44
Matthew 19: 12
Matthew 22: 37–39
Matthew 25: 35
Matthew 25: 36
Luke 19: 9, 10

Luke 23: 33
John 3: 16
John 13: 35
John 15: 9
John 15: 13
Romans 5: 8
Romans 7: 19
1 Corinthians 6: 13
1 Corinthians 7: 5
1 Corinthians 13: 3
1 Corinthians 13: 13
1 Timothy 1: 16
2 Timothy 1: 5
Hebrews 13: 2
James 2: 14–17
James 4: 1
1 Peter 2: 20
1 John 3: 1
1 John 3: 16
1 John 4: 10
1 John 4: 16
1 John 5: 13